W9-DJM-465

This book is dedicated to
my grandchildren
Freddy, Lauren, Jeremy, and Joy
four precious gifts from God

Spiritual Gifts

by Renald E. Showers

Spiritual Gifts

© 2007 Renald E. Showers

Published by Renald E. Showers

Scripture quotations are taken from the King James Version of the Holy Bible.

ISBN 978-1-880976-50-0

TABLE OF CONTENTS

INTRODUCTION

For quite a few years sincere Christians have struggled with several significant issues related to the subject of spiritual gifts. What is a spiritual gift? How can a person discern what gift or gifts he or she has been given? Is there a relationship between the possession of spiritual gifts and spirituality? Did God intend the gifts possessed by the early Church to remain in the Church throughout its history? These and other related issues will be addressed in this booklet.

SPIRITUAL GIFTS— THEIR DEFINITION, DISCERNMENT, AND PURPOSE

A Definition of a Spiritual Gift

As one examines everything which is stated in the Scriptures concerning spiritual gifts (the lists of gifts, their purposes, etc.), it becomes rather obvious that spiritual gifts are God-given abilities to minister or serve. This will be noted quite clearly when the purpose of spiritual gifts is considered later.

In addition, the Scriptures indicate that the gifts are given to believers by the Holy Spirit (1 Cor. 12:7–11) and that the giving of a spiritual gift is an act of God's grace (the major part of the word which is translated "gifts" is the New Testament word for "grace," compare Rom. 12:6 and 1 Pet. 4:10).

In light of these various factors a spiritual gift could be defined as follows: A spiritual gift is a particular ability to minister to other people which is given graciously by the Holy Spirit to a believer.

The Discernment of Spiritual Gifts

Since spiritual gifts are God-given abilities to minister, they are designed to determine the ministry or ministries which a believer is to have. Inasmuch as spiritual gifts determine ministry, it is essential that each believer discern what gift or gifts he or she possesses.

How can one discern which gifts are possessed? When three different criteria line up in agreement with each other to point in the same direction, that alignment is a good indicator of how a person has been gifted. Those three criteria are as follows: First, what does the believer really enjoy doing by way of ministry? Usually a person enjoys doing what he or she is capable of doing. It is a chore to perform a ministry for which a person has not been given ability. Thus, the genuine enjoyment of a particular kind of ministry is a good indicator of the ability which has been given to a person.

The second criterion is: What particular ability or abilities to minister do other believers recognize in a person? The body of Christ can play a key role in the discernment of possessed spiritual gifts by observing the individual believer and then pointing out recognized abilities.

The third criterion is: In which particular ministries is the person most effective? Certainly a believer will be most effective in those kinds of ministries for which the Spirit has given special abilities. Thus, effectiveness can also be a good indicator of how a person has been gifted.

The Purpose of Spiritual Gifts

Every spiritual gift is given for the purpose of enabling the gift possessor to minister to others, *not* to minister to himself. Thus, a spiritual gift is given for the benefit of others, not for the benefit of the one having the gift.

Several things in the Scriptures indicate that this is so. First, in 1 Corinthians 12:7 Paul stated that each believer is given a gift of the Spirit "to profit withal." The immediate context (vv. 12–27 where Paul emphasized that every believer is essential to the proper functioning of the Church and that believers should care for one another) and the remote context (10:24, 33 where Paul stressed the importance of believers seeking, not their own profit, but the profit of the many) of Paul's statement indicate that, when he said that a spiritual gift is given "to profit withal," he had in mind the profit of many other people, not the profit of the one who possesses the gift.

Second, Paul inserted the greatest chapter on love (1 Cor. 13) in the center of the most extensive biblical passage dealing with the subject of spiritual gifts (1 Cor. 12–14). The Spirit of God had a specific reason for moving the apostle to emphasize love in the middle of his great discourse on spiritual gifts. The reason was that the Corinthian Christians had been using their gifts for their own selfish benefit. Their attitude concerning the purpose of the spiritual gifts was wrong. Paul was determined to correct that attitude by stressing the importance of love, which is the attitude of being more concerned for the welfare of others than for one's own welfare (Jn. 15:13; Rom. 5:8; 2 Cor. 8:9; Phil. 2:1–8; 1 Jn. 3:16). Thus, he declared that love does not seek its own benefit (1 Cor. 13:5). The apostle wanted the Corinthian Christians to see that they had been given their spiritual gifts for the benefit of others, not for their own benefit.

Third, in 1 Peter 4:10 Peter wrote the following: "As every man hath received the gift, even so minister the same one to another, as good stewards of the manifold grace of God." The article "the" before the word "gift" is not found in the Greek text of Peter's statement. Thus, Peter said: "As every man hath received a gift" and thereby indicated that every believer has been given at least one spiritual gift.

Peter stated that believers are stewards of the spiritual gifts which are entrusted to them by God's grace. This means that God holds believers responsible to exercise their gifts in accord with their God-intended purpose.

The apostle declared that believers are to use their spiritual gifts to minister to one another. This indicates that the God-intended purpose of every spiritual gift is to enable the gift possessor to serve others. The use of a gift for any other purpose is a violation of the stewardship entrusted to the believer.

Some would consider this stated purpose of spiritual gifts to be a contradiction of Paul's statement in 1 Corinthians 14:4. In that passage the apostle declared that the believer who speaks in a tongue edifies himself. On the basis of that statement some believers, who claim to have the gift of tongues, are convinced that it is legitimate to use that gift for the purpose of self-edification. They claim that they exercise the gift of tongues only in their private devotions for their own spiritual edification.

Several things should be noted, however, concerning Paul's statement in 1 Corinthians 14:4. First, in the context Paul was talking about the exercise of the gift of tongues in a public church worship service, not in private (vv. 4–6, 9, 12 indicate this). Thus, the passage is not dealing with the use of the gift in private, and Paul was neither approving nor advocating speaking in tongues in private.

Second, a close examination of Paul's statement and its context indicates that the apostle was actually rebuking the Corinthian Christians for exercising the gift of tongues in a way that did not benefit others. Paul was saying that the gift of tongues should never be exercised in a church worship service apart from the exercise of the gift of interpretation, because by itself the gift of tongues would never edify the rest of the church. Others in the church would not benefit, because the tongues speaking would be foreign to them. God would understand what was said through the tongues speaking, for God understands all languages, but other people in the church would not understand (vv. 2, 5–6, 9, 11–13, 16–19). In light of this rebuke, Paul was neither approving nor advocating speaking in tongues for the purpose of self-edification.

Actually the use of the gift of tongues in private for one's own edification would be wrong for several reasons. First, such usage would violate the God-intended purpose for all spiritual gifts in general. As noted earlier, the purpose of all spiritual gifts is to enable the gift possessors to minister to others. Private tongues speaking for self-edification would not be a ministry to other people.

Second, such usage would violate love, which is the attitude of being more concerned for the welfare of others than for one's own welfare. As noted earlier, Paul wrote his great chapter on love in the middle of his extensive discourse on spiritual gifts, because he wanted the Corinthian Christians to see that they had been given their spiritual gifts for the benefit of others, not for their own benefit. Private tongues speaking for self-edification would be a selfish exercise of the gift, not an expression of love.

Third, such usage would violate the specific purpose of the

gift of tongues. Only one passage in the Bible identified the specific purpose of the gift of tongues. In 1 Corinthians 14:22 Paul wrote: "Wherefore, tongues are for a sign." The apostle thereby indicated that God intended tongues to be a sign gift, not an edification gift. Private tongues speaking for self-edification would be an attempt to use tongues as an edification gift, not as a sign gift. This would be contrary to God's intended purpose.

In addition, the New Testament usage of the word which is translated "sign" (it is also translated "miracle") indicates that signs are intended to be public, to be seen by numbers of people. For example, the New Testament talks about signs appearing (Mt. 24:30), being shown (Mk. 13:22), being seen (Jn. 2:23; 6:2, 14; Acts 8:6, 13) and being done before people (Jn. 12:37), in the midst of people (Acts 2:22) and among people (Acts 15:12; 2 Cor. 12:12). Thus, signs are designed to enable the sign performer to communicate something to others. The very nature, purpose and function of a sign demand that it be public. In light of this, since God intended tongues to be a sign, then that gift was always to be exercised in public, not in private.

Fourth, private tongues speaking for self-edification of the believer would violate the God-intended beneficiaries of the gift. In 1 Corinthians 14:22 Paul said: "Wherefore, tongues are for a sign, not to them that believe, but to them that believe not." Tongues speaking was to be a sign of something to unbelievers, not to believers. The apostle, therefore, was asserting that God intended the gift of tongues to benefit unbelievers, not believers. The private use of the gift by a believer for his own benefit would not benefit unbelievers.

Some would declare that this understanding of the specific purpose of the gift of tongues is in conflict with Paul's statement in Romans 8:26. There the apostle wrote: "Likewise, the Spirit also helpeth our infirmity; for we know not what we should pray for as we ought; but the Spirit himself maketh intercession for us with groanings which cannot be uttered." On the basis of that statement some believers, who claim to have the gift of tongues, assert that, when they speak in tongues in private devotions, it is the Holy Spirit who is controlling them and praying through and for them with a prayer language in fulfillment of Romans 8:26.

There is a major problem, however, with this approach to and understanding of Romans 8:26. The word in Paul's statement which is translated "which cannot be uttered" means "unexpressed, wordless."[1] It is related to the word which means "mute, dumb."[2] A very literal translation of the root of both words is "no speaking." The meaning of these terms indicates that Paul was referring to a totally silent praying of the Holy Spirit on behalf of believers. This praying involves no sound audible to the human ear. By contrast the biblical gift of tongues did involve audible sound. Otherwise it could not be a sign to unbelievers.

Endnotes

[1] William F. Arndt and F. Wilbur Gingrich, "alaletos," *A Greek-English Lexicon Of The New Testament* (4th rev. ed.; Chicago: The University of Chicago Press, 1957), p. 34.
[2] "alaletos," Ibid.

SPIRITUAL GIFTS–
THEIR DISTRIBUTION AND
RELATIONSHIPS

The Sovereign Distribution
of Spiritual Gifts

Although Paul told the Corinthian Christians to "covet earnestly the best gifts" (1 Cor. 12:31; cf. 14:1), he made it clear that the Holy Spirit distributes the gifts according to His sovereign will. After having listed several different gifts which the Spirit gave to believers (1 Cor. 12:8–10), Paul declared, "But all these worketh that one and the very same Spirit, dividing to every man severally as he will" (1 Cor. 12:11; cf. 12:18).

The fact that the Holy Spirit distributes spiritual gifts according to His sovereign will indicates several things. First, believers have no guarantee that they will receive the specific spiritual gifts which they desire. The reception of gifts is determined ultimately, not by their desire or seeking, but by the Spirit's will. Second, Christians cannot obligate or force the Spirit to give them certain gifts. Third, there are no magic formulas, no planned schemes, no set procedures which believers can devise or employ to obtain specific gifts. Nowhere do the Scriptures teach or propose the development of such manmade, artificial gimmicks for the purpose of receiving genuine spiritual gifts. Instead, the Scriptures indicate that the reception of gifts is governed by the Spirit's choice and that He determines to give every believer at least one gift (1 Cor. 12:11; 1 Pet. 4:10).

Limitations Upon the Distribution of Spiritual Gifts

The Scriptures present at least two significant limitations which God has placed upon the distribution of spiritual gifts. First, God never gives one particular gift to all believers. Paul indicated this in 1 Corinthians 12:8–10 where he declared that the Spirit gives one kind of gift to one believer and a different kind of gift to another believer.

The obvious reason for this limitation is the fact that God does not want all believers to have the same ministry. The body of Christ, the Church, would be lopsided in ministry if God were to give every believer the same gift. Paul declared, "If the whole body were an eye, where were the hearing? If the whole were hearing, where were the smelling?" (1 Cor. 12:17). Just as God designed the human body to have several members with different functions, so He designed the body of Christ, the Church, to have many members with different ministries. Paul said, "For the body is not one member, but many" (1 Cor. 12:14, cf. v. 12), and "But now hath God set the members, every one of them, in the body, as it hath pleased him. And if they were all one member, where were the body?" (1 Cor. 12:18–19). If all believers had the same spiritual gift, then the Church really would not function as a body.

In order to emphasize the fact that God does not give one particular gift to all believers, Paul asked the following series of questions in 1 Corinthians 12:29–30: "Are all apostles? Are all prophets? Are all teachers? Are all workers of miracles? Have all the gifts of healing? Do all speak with tongues? Do all interpret?" In the original New Testament there was more than one way of asking a question. One of those ways implied a "no" answer to the question.[1] Paul used this specific way in every one of his questions in verses 29–30. Thus, every one of those questions implied a "no" answer, and Paul was thereby indicating that God does not give the same gift to all believers.

It is important to note that one of Paul's questions which implied a "no" answer was, "Do all speak with tongues?" The required negative answer to this specific question indicated that the gift of tongues was subject to the same limitation which God placed upon the distribution of all spiritual gifts. Thus, even in apostolic times God never gave the gift of tongues to every believer. He purposely refused to do so, so that the New Testament Church would not be lopsided in its ministry. It was wrong, therefore, for every believer to expect to speak in tongues.

Since God gave the gift of salvation to every true believer but refused to give the gift of tongues to every believer, it can be concluded that God never intended speaking in tongues to be a sign of salvation. Earlier it was noted that the purpose of every spiritual gift is to enable the gift possessor to minister to others, not to minister to himself. Thus, the God-ordained purpose of the gift of tongues was not that of assuring the tongues speaker of his salvation.

The second limitation which God has placed upon the distribution of spiritual gifts is as follows: God never gives all the spiritual gifts to one believer. This limitation was also implied in 1 Corinthians 12:8–10 where Paul declared that the Spirit gives different gifts to different believers.

God purposely refuses to give all the gifts to one believer because He does not want a self-sufficient "Super Saint" who has no need for the ministries and fellowship of other believers. Paul wrote, "And the eye cannot say unto the hand, I have no need of thee: nor again the head to the feet, I have no need of you. Nay, much more those members of the body which seem to be more feeble, are necessary" (1 Cor. 12:21–22). God intentionally distributes the gifts in such a way that believers need each other and care for each other. God does not want Christians to be "loners" who divide themselves from the rest of the body of Christ. Paul expressed it this way—"That there should be no schism in the body, but that the members should have the same care one for another" (1 Cor. 12:25). In other words, God has designed the spiritual gifts to be a source of unity, rather than a source of division, for the Church.

The Relationship of the
Gift of Tongues to Spirit Baptism

On the day of His ascension Jesus indicated that His apostles would be baptized with the Holy Spirit in a few more days

(Acts 1:5). When that promise was fulfilled on the Day of Pentecost, the apostles spoke in tongues (Acts 2:4). On another occasion, Cornelius and the members of his household spoke in tongues when the Holy Spirit was poured out on them while Peter spoke (Acts 10:44–46). Later Peter indicated that Cornelius and the others had been baptized with the Spirit on that occasion (Acts 11:15–16).

In light of these incidents in which Spirit baptism and speaking in tongues took place at the same time, some sincere Christians have concluded that Spirit baptism involves the reception of either the Holy Spirit or His supernatural empowerment, that Spirit baptism may happen to a believer sometime after salvation, that tongues speaking is the sign that one has received Spirit baptism and that any believer who has not spoken in tongues has not received Spirit baptism. Because of these conclusions, some Christians zealously press other believers to seek "the baptism" by speaking in tongues.

The key biblical passage on Spirit baptism is opposed to these conclusions and actions. The only passage which identifies the significance, recipients and time of Spirit baptism is 1 Corinthians 12:13. Paul declared, "For by one Spirit were we all baptized into one body, whether we be Jews or Greeks, whether we be bond or free; and have been all made to drink into one Spirit."

Paul's declaration indicates several significant things concerning Spirit baptism. First, it indicates that every believer has received Spirit baptism ("by one Spirit were we all baptized"). That this is so is supported by the fact that the Scriptures never urge or command believers to be baptized with the Spirit or to seek Spirit baptism. Indeed, nowhere do the Scriptures record believers seeking this baptism. It is senseless to seek for something which has already happened.

Second, Paul's declaration indicates the time of Spirit baptism. Since every believer has received Spirit baptism, it can be concluded that Spirit baptism happens at the moment of salvation. If it were to happen sometime after salvation, then Paul could not have said that all believers have been baptized with the Spirit. Some would have been baptized; others would have not by the time of Paul's statement. Since all believers receive Spirit baptism at the time of salvation, it is wrong for some Christians to press other believers to seek "the baptism."

Third, Paul's declaration indicates the significance of Spirit baptism. It has the significance of placing the believer into the body of Christ, the Church ("by one Spirit were we all baptized into one body"), not the significance of supernatural empowerment. In the context of his 1 Corinthians 12:13 declaration, Paul drew analogy between the body of Christ, the church, and the human body (vv.12–18). Just as the human body is only one body even though it has many members, so the body of Christ is only one body even though it has many members.

In 1 Corinthians 12:13 Paul told how believers at salvation are put into the one body of Christ to become its members. It happens through Spirit baptism. In other words, Spirit baptism is that work of God which builds or forms the body of Christ, the Church.

An important contrast should be observed between Paul's teaching in 1 Corinthians 12:13 and that in 1 Corinthians 12:30. In 1 Corinthians 12:13 Paul taught that every believer had been baptized with the Spirit, but, as noted earlier, in 1 Corinthians 12:30 he indicated that God refused to give the gift of tongues to every believer. Thus, in Paul's day all believers had been baptized with the Spirit, but many were never given the ability to speak in tongues. The fact that God gave every believer Spirit baptism but refused to give every believer the gift of tongues indicates that tongues speaking was *not* to be the sign that one had received Spirit baptism. In order for it to be such a sign, every believer would have to speak in tongues, since every believer had been baptized with the Spirit. Thus, it is wrong to conclude that any believer who has not spoken in tongues has not received Spirit baptism.

Some would object to this conclusion by insisting that the New Testament draws a distinction between baptism *by* the Spirit and baptism *with* the Spirit. They would assert that these are two different Spirit baptisms with two different significances. According to this approach, baptism *by* the Spirit (1 Cor. 12:13) places every believer into the body of Christ at the moment of salvation, but baptism *with* the Spirit (Acts 1:5; 11:15–16) gives supernatural empowerment, is accompanied by speaking in tongues (Acts 2:4; 10:44–46) and can take place after salvation. Thus, tongues speaking *would* be a sign that one had been baptized *with* the Spirit.

This approach has a major problem, however. It is based upon an English translation of the passages dealing with Spirit baptism, not upon the Greek text of the New Testament. Although English translations have used two different English prepositions ("by" and "with") to translate the passages dealing with Spirit baptism, the Greek text always used the same Greek preposition for every New Testament reference to Spirit baptism. This indicates that the original New Testament consistently recognized and presented only one kind of Spirit baptism (that which places every believer into the body of Christ, the Church).

The Relationship of
Spiritual Gifts to Spirituality

The possession and exercise of spiritual gifts do not make a believer spiritual. In addition, the possession and exercise of spiritual gifts are not a sign of spirituality. The Corinthian Christians clearly demonstrated the truthfulness of these statements. On the one hand, as a group they possessed and exercised all the spiritual gifts which the Holy Spirit gave to the early Christians (1 Cor. 1:7). But, on the other hand, Paul declared that they were not spiritual (1 Cor. 3:1–3).

There is a definite distinction between the possession and exercise of a spiritual gift and spirituality. The possession and exercise of a spiritual gift are the result of the Holy Spirit giving the believer a particular ability to minister to other people. Spirituality is the result of the Holy Spirit controlling the life of the believer. The possession and exercise of a spiritual gift relate primarily to what the believer does in the realm of ministry. Spirituality relates primarily to what the believer is and does in the realm of character. The possession and exercise of a spiritual gift produce a ministry impact upon the lives of others. Spirituality produces a godly character which is characterized by the fruit of the Holy Spirit (love, joy, peace, long-suffering, gentleness, goodness, faith, meekness, self-control—Gal. 5:22–23). It also produces a godly lifestyle which is characterized by purity and obedience to God (Gal. 5:16–21).

In light of the facts that the Corinthian Christians possessed and exercised numerous spiritual gifts and yet were not spiritual, and that there is a definite distinction between the possession and exercise of a spiritual gift and spirituality, two major conclusions can be drawn. First, a Christian does not have to be spiritual in order to possess and exercise a spiritual gift. In other words, a godly character and pure, obedient lifestyle are not required in order to possess and exercise a spiritual gift. This has frightening implications, for it means that a believer can perform a ministry even when his character and conduct are not what they should be. This explains, then, why some pastors, Bible teachers and television evangelists have the ability to continue their ministries in spite of the fact that they are involved in illicit affairs and pursuing extravagant lifestyles.

Second, the possession and exercise of spiritual gifts cannot be made a test of spirituality. As noted earlier, spirituality is associated with the fruit of the Spirit, which includes love (Gal. 5:22–23), but Paul indicated that it was possible for a believer to do such things as speak in tongues and prophesy without having love (1 Cor. 13:1–3). In other words, a believer can possess and exercise spiritual gifts without being spiritual. Since a believer can possess and exercise spiritual gifts without being spiritual, it is wrong to make the possession and exercise of any spiritual gift a test of spirituality. Christians, therefore, should never make such a thing as speaking in tongues a test of spirituality. The true test of spirituality is as follows: Is the believer's life characterized by the fruit of the Spirit, purity and obedience to God?

Endnote

[1] H. E. Dana and Julius R. Mantey, *A Manual Grammar of the Greek New Testament* (New York: The Macmillan Co., 1927), p. 265.

SPIRITUAL GIFTS— THEIR DURATION

A Significant Disagreement

Sincere Christians disagree with each other concerning the issue of the duration of spiritual gifts. Some believe that God intended all the gifts possessed by the early Church to remain in the Church throughout its history. Others believe that God intended some of the gifts to be temporary—to exist in the Church just during the time of the apostles of Jesus Christ (during the first century A.D.). Those who advocate the latter view normally assert that it was the revelational and sign gifts which were to be temporary.

It is important to note that the heart of the disagreement is related to the intention of God, not to the authority and power of God. Certainly God has the authority and power to do whatever He wants, whenever He wants. Thus, the real issue is not God's ability to continue all the spiritual gifts throughout the history of the Church. Instead, it is God's intention. Did God intend to make all the gifts permanent in the Church, or did He intend to make some temporary?

Evidence for the Temporary Nature of Some Gifts

There is reason to believe that God intended some of the spiritual gifts which He gave to the early Church to be temporary. The Scriptures present several lines of evidence to that effect.

First, the apostles of Christ were temporary, and some of the spiritual gifts were unique to them. Certain biblical factors indicate that the apostles of Christ were temporary. First, in order to be an apostle of Christ (in contrast with mere apostles of churches—2 Cor. 8:23 where "messengers" is a translation of the word "apostles"; Phil. 2:25), one normally was required to have been with Christ throughout His entire earthly ministry. Peter stated this requirement in Acts 1:21–22. Paul was the one exception to this normal requirement. For that reason, he stated that he was "born out of due time" (1 Cor. 15:8), and some challenged his claim to be an apostle of Christ (2 Cor. 12:11). In light of this normal requirement, it is apparent that people of later generations did not qualify to be an apostle of Christ. Rengstorf wrote: "It is only logical that the apostolate should be limited to the first generation and should not become an ecclesiastical office."[1]

Second, in order to be an apostle of Christ, one had to have seen the resurrected Christ with his own eyes (1 Cor. 9:1). The reason for this requirement was as follows: One of the major responsibilities of an apostle of Christ was to give eyewitness testimony to the fact that Jesus Christ rose bodily from the dead (Lk. 24:46–48; Acts 1:8; 2:32; 3:15; 5:29–32; 10:39–42; 13:30–31).

In light of this requirement, Paul's statement in 1 Corinthians 15:8 is most significant. After referring to Christ's post-resurrection appearance to all the apostles, he declared: "And last of all he was seen of me also, as of one born out of due time." In light of the fact that Christ appeared to the Apostle John on the Island of Patmos several years after His appearance to Paul, one must conclude that the appearance to Paul was not the absolute last post-resurrection appearance by Christ. Instead, it must have been the last one for the purpose of making a person an apostle of Christ.

Thus, Grosheide wrote:

Paul directly joins the appearance of Christ to himself to the one to all the apostles: *and last of all—He appeared unto me. Last of all:* the last one in this series. Paul was the last one to see the glorified Lord with his own eyes, in order that he might be a true apostle. Hence the words: *the child untimely born.* The article before *child* shows us how Paul designates himself in relation to the other apostles.[2]

Paul's statement, then, strongly implies that he was the last person to be made an apostle of Christ.

Third, neither the Scriptures nor church history records indicate that new apostles of Christ were appointed by God or the Church after Paul to replace the first generation apostles as they departed through death. Certainly God would have appointed replacements if He had intended the Church to have apostles of Christ throughout its history.

Fourth, in Ephesians 2:20, where Paul drew an analogy between the construction of a building and the construction of the Church, he declared that the apostles and New Testament prophets are the foundation of the Church. Since the foundation of a building is laid once and for all in the early stages of construction, Paul's analogy implies that the apostles were present once and for all in the early stages of the Church. Just as the foundation is not built up to the top of a building, so apostles of Christ are not present in the Church throughout its history.

There are good reasons, then, for concluding that there were no more apostles of Christ after John, the last of the first generation apostles to die, departed this life around 100 A.D. The apostles of Christ were temporary. They were limited to the first century of the Church's existence.

In light of the fact that apostles of Christ were temporary, Paul's statement in 2 Corinthians 12:12 is most significant. Some opponents had been attacking the validity of Paul's apostleship (v. 11). In order to demonstrate the fact that he was a true apostle of Christ, Paul stated: "Truly the signs of an apostle were wrought among you in all patience, in signs, and wonders, and mighty deeds" (v. 12). Paul's statement indicates that some of the miraculous sign gifts in the early Church were unique to the apostles. In other words, some of the sign gifts were possessed and exercised just by the apostles of Christ, not by any other believers.

Those specific sign gifts had the function of identifying apostles of Christ in contrast with other believers. If this had not been so, then those gifts would not have been "the signs of an apostle," and Paul could not have used them as proof that he was a true apostle of Christ (cf. Acts 2:43; Heb. 2:3–4). Rengstorf indicated that such miraculous action by an apostle of Christ "is essential, for in it the messenger has and gives proof that he is really the commissioned representative of Jesus."[3]

Since the apostles of Christ were temporary, and since some of the sign gifts were unique to them, then it can be concluded that those particular spiritual gifts which were unique to the apostles were also temporary. Since those gifts had the function of identifying apostles of Christ, once the apostles were gone, those gifts had no further purpose to exist. They ceased when the apostles of Christ ceased. God did not intend those particular gifts to be permanent in the Church.

A second line of evidence to the effect that God intended some of the spiritual gifts which He gave to the early Church to be temporary is as follows: *The Apostle Paul specifically declared that some of the gifts were temporary.* In 1 Corinthians 13:8 Paul, writing under the supernatural influence of the Holy Spirit, stated: "whether there be prophecies, they shall be done away; whether there be tongues, they shall cease; whether there be knowledge, it shall vanish away." Since Paul made this declaration in the midst of his most extensive discourse on spiritual gifts, it can be concluded that the apostle was referring to the spiritual gifts of prophecy, tongues and knowledge.

Paul made this statement as part of a line of thought. He developed this line of thought in the following manner. First, he asserted that love is superior to the spiritual gifts (1 Cor. 12:31–13:7). Then he gave one of the reasons for love being superior to the gifts (v. 8). Love is superior to the spiritual gifts because love never fails; it is permanent; it abides (cf. v. 13). By contrast, *some* of the spiritual gifts are temporary. They will fail, will cease, will vanish away.

The apostle named three specific spiritual gifts (prophecy, tongues, knowledge) as examples of those which were temporary. The specific gifts which Paul named belonged to two different categories of gifts. Prophecy and knowledge belonged to the category of revelational gifts. According to Paul's statement in 1 Corinthians 14:22, tongues belonged to the category of sign gifts. It would appear, then, that Paul was indicating that the revelational and sign gifts were temporary.

Next in his line of thought Paul gave an example of why some of the spiritual gifts were temporary: "For we know in part, and we prophesy in part" (v. 9). Using as his example the two revelational gifts of prophecy and knowledge to which he had referred in verse eight, Paul presented the following teaching in verse nine: The revelational gifts were temporary because they delivered only a partial revelation or knowledge of God. That was their God intended purpose or function. They were not capable of delivering a full, complete revelation or knowledge of God. Thus, once the revelational gifts had delivered all of the partial revelation or knowledge of God which they were capable of delivering, they had fulfilled their God-intended purpose or function and were no longer necessary. Because they had fulfilled their intended purpose or function and were no longer necessary, God did away with them.

It is important to note that, through this example of why some of the spiritual gifts were temporary, Paul indicated a significant principle concerning spiritual gifts. That principle is as follows: It is the purpose or function of a spiritual gift that determines its duration. A spiritual gift will continue to exist until it fulfills its God-intended purpose or function. But once it fulfills its intended purpose or function, it is no longer necessary, and God does away with it.

Did Paul state the specific time when the revelational gifts would fulfill their intended purpose or function and thereby be put out of existence? Some believe that he did in 1 Corinthians 13:10. After having stated, "For we know in part, and we prophesy in part" (v. 9), Paul went on to assert, "But when that which is perfect is come, then that which is in part shall be done away" (v. 10). Those who believe that in verse ten Paul stated the specific time when the revelational gifts would be abolished are convinced that the expression "that which is in part" in verse ten refers to the spiritual gifts. Thus, they think that Paul said that the spiritual gifts would be done away when the perfect comes.

There is a major problem with this view, however. The expression "that which is in part" cannot refer to the spiritual gifts. It cannot for at least two reasons. First, there is no such thing as a partial gift. Second, in the Greek text of verse ten the term which is translated "that which" is singular in number. By contrast, in the immediately preceding context (v. 9) Paul referred to two spiritual gifts (plural), the gifts of prophecy and knowledge. Since a noun or pronoun is required to agree in number with its antecedent, and since the expression "that which" (v. 10) is singular in number and the spiritual gifts (v. 9) are plural in number, then the expression "that which is in part" (v. 10) cannot be referring to the spiritual gifts. Thus, Paul was *not* saying that the spiritual gifts would be done away when the perfect would come (v. 10).

If the expression "that which is in part" (v. 10) cannot refer to the spiritual gifts, to what then does it refer? The Greek words which are translated "in part" in verse ten are the same as those translated "in part" in verse nine. It seems apparent that they are referring to the same thing in both verses. Earlier it was noted that in verse nine those words referred to the partial revelation or knowledge of God which the revelational gifts were capable of delivering. Thus, it seems apparent that the expression "that which is in part" in verse ten is also referring to the partial revelation or knowledge of God which came through the revelational gifts.

The Greek word which is translated "perfect" in the expression "that which is perfect" (v. 10) means *whole*, *complete* or *total*.[4] It is the opposite of the expression "in part."[5] Thus, it refers to the full, complete revelation or knowledge of God in contrast with the partial revelation or knowledge of God which the revelational gifts were able to deliver.[6]

An important distinction should be noted at this point. There is a difference between the revelational gifts which could deliver the partial revelation or knowledge of God *and* the partial revelation or knowledge of God which was delivered through the revelational gifts. The two are not the same. The gifts were the cause of the partial revelation or knowledge, *and* the partial revelation or knowledge was the result of the gifts.

In light of this distinction and what has been seen about the meaning of expressions in verse ten, the following conclusion can be drawn: In 1 Corinthians 13:10 Paul was *not* stating the time when the revelational gifts would be done away. Instead, he *was* stating the time when the partial revelation or knowledge of God which came through those gifts would be done away. He was *not* declaring that the spiritual gifts would be done away when that which is perfect would come. Instead, he *was* declaring that the partial revelation or knowledge of God which came through the revelational gifts would be done away when the full, complete revelation or knowledge of God would come.

In spite of the fact that in 1 Corinthians 13:8 Paul clearly indicated that revelational and sign gifts were temporary, neither in verse ten nor any other verse of chapter thirteen did he state the time when those gifts would end. Other Scriptures indicate when they would terminate. Those other Scriptures will be examined in the next chapter.

A third line of evidence to the effect that God intended some of the spiritual gifts which He gave to the early Church to be temporary is found in Hebrews 6:5. In that passage the Holy Spirit moved the writer to refer to the miracles performed by Jesus and His apostles as "the powers of the world to come" (literally, "the age to come"). Since Hebrews was written during this present age, the expression "the age to come" is a reference to the next great age of this earth's history—the coming Millennial Age, when Messiah will administer God's Kingdom rule over the entire earth (Dan. 2:44; 7:13–14, 27; Zech. 14:9). Thus, the writer of Hebrews was calling the miracles of Jesus and His apostles "the powers of the future Millennial Age."

Jesus possessed and exercised great miraculous powers during His first coming (Mt. 9). He gave those same miraculous powers to His apostles to exercise (Mt. 10:1–4). It is significant to note that Jesus exercised His miraculous powers in conjunction with His proclamation of "the gospel of the kingdom" (Mt. 9:35). He also commanded His apostles to exercise those same miraculous powers in conjunction with their proclamation of the same kingdom message exclusively to the people of Israel (Mt. 10:5–8; Lk. 9:1–2).

A comparison of the miracles performed by Jesus and His apostles with Old Testament prophecies concerning the miraculous changes which Messiah will bring to the world when He establishes the Kingdom of God in the future Millennial Age indicates two things. First, the miracles performed by Jesus and His apostles were a foretaste, a sampling, of the miraculous changes which will characterize the future Millennial Age when Messiah will establish and rule over the Kingdom of God on earth (Mt. 19:28; Acts 3:19–21). Second, the ultimate purpose of the miracles performed by Jesus and the apostles was to demonstrate the fact that Jesus of Nazareth is the promised Messiah, the One who can and will establish the Kingdom of God of the future Millennial Age when the people of Israel repent (Lk. 7:19–23; Jn. 10:24–25; 12:37; 20:30–31; Acts 2:22, 36; Heb. 2:3–4).[7]

It was because of this twofold significance of the miracles of Jesus and His apostles, plus the fact that they performed their miracles in conjunction with their proclamation of the gospel of the Kingdom, that the Holy Spirit moved the writer of Hebrews to call the miracles of Jesus and His apostles "the powers of the future Millennial Age." This was the Holy Spirit's way of indicating that the miraculous powers of Jesus and His apostles were uniquely related to the future Millennial Age. They were to be characteristic of that age, not of the present age. As a result, those miraculous powers were not to be present throughout this present age. If they were to be present throughout this present age, then they would be "the powers of this age," not "the powers of the age to come." Thus, Hebrews 6:5 implies that the miraculous sign gifts which belonged to the apostles of Christ were temporary. God did not intend them to continue throughout this present age.

ENDNOTES

[1] Karl Heinrich Rengstorf, "apostolos," *Theological Dictionary of the New Testament,* Vol. I (Grand Rapids: Wm. B. Eerdmans Publishing Co., 1964), p. 432.

[2] F. W. Grosheide, "Commentary On The First Epistle To The Corinthians," of *The New International Commentary on the New Testament* (Grand Rapids: Wm. B. Eerdmans Publishing Co., 1953), p. 352.

[3] Rengstorf, "apostolos," p. 429.

[4] Gerhard Delling, "teleios," *Theological Dictionary of the New Testament*, Vol. VIII (Grand Rapids: Wm. B. Eerdmans Publishing Co., 1972), p. 74.

[5] Ibid., p. 75.

[6] Ibid.

[7] For a study of these two indications see: Renald E. Showers, "The Purpose of Jesus' Miracles," *Israel My Glory*, December/January, 1975–76.

THE CESSATION OF REVELATIONAL GIFTS

The previous chapter on spiritual gifts dealt with several significant factors. First, it presented three lines of evidence to the effect that God intended the revelational and sign gifts which He gave to the early Church to be temporary.

Second, it noted a significant principle concerning spiritual gifts. That principle is as follows: The duration of a spiritual gift is determined by its purpose or function. A spiritual gift will continue to exist until it fulfills its God-intended purpose or function. Once it fulfills that purpose or function, it is no longer necessary, and God does away with it.

In light of these significant factors already examined, this chapter will study more specifically the issue of when some of the spiritual gifts which God intended to be temporary actually ended.

The Duration of Revelational Gifts

On the basis of Paul's statements in 1 Corinthians 13:8–9, the previous chapter noted several things concerning the duration of the revelational gifts of prophecy and knowledge. First, in contrast with love which is permanent, the gifts of prophecy and knowledge would be temporary. They would fail, would vanish away.

Second, the revelational gifts of prophecy and knowledge would be temporary because they could deliver only a partial revelation or knowledge of God. That was their God-intended purpose or function. They were not capable of delivering a full, complete revelation of God.

Third, in line with the principle noted earlier to the effect that the duration of a spiritual gift is determined by its purpose or function, once the revelational gifts would have delivered all of the partial revelation or knowledge of God which they were capable of delivering, they would have fulfilled their God-intended purpose or function and would no longer be necessary. Thus, God would do away with them.

In light of these three items concerning the duration of the revelational gifts of prophecy and knowledge, the following questions must be asked: According to the Holy Spirit-inspired Scriptures, when would the revelational gifts of prophecy and knowledge fulfill their God-intended purpose or function of delivering all of the partial revelation or knowledge of God which they were capable of delivering? And when, therefore, would God do away with those gifts?

These questions were not answered by Paul in 1 Corinthians 13. The previous chapter demonstrated the fact that, although he clearly taught the temporary duration of the revelational gifts of prophecy and knowledge in verse eight, nowhere in chapter thirteen did Paul state the specific time when those revelational gifts would fulfill their intended purpose or function and thereby be put out of existence.

Three other Scripture passages do shed significant light on these issues. The first of these passages is John 14:26. In the context of this passage Jesus had gathered with His twelve apostles in the upper room in Jerusalem on the night before His crucifixion. Jesus warned the apostles that He would be leaving them to return to His Father's house in Heaven (Jn. 14:1–3). He promised His men that they would not be left alone during His absence. The Father would send to them another Comforter in place of Jesus (v. 16). That other Comforter would be the Holy Spirit (v. 17; cf. Jn. 7:39).

Having promised the coming of the Holy Spirit to His apostles, Jesus told them what the Spirit would do after He would come— "But the Comforter, who is the Holy Spirit, whom the Father will send in my name, he shall teach you all things" (Jn. 14:26).

Several important things should be noted concerning this significant statement by Jesus. First, it is important to note to whom Jesus addressed this statement. He addressed it specifically to the twelve apostles, not to all believers in general. That this is so is indicated by the rest of Jesus' statement in verse twenty-six. Having promised that the Holy Spirit would teach these men all things, Jesus then declared that the Spirit would also "bring all things to your remembrance, whatever I have said unto you." Only the apostles had been with Jesus during all the times that He had taught; therefore, only they had heard all of His instruction. Thus, in John 14:26 Jesus was talking about significant things which the Holy Spirit would do to that corporate body of apostles during their corporate lifetime. He was not indicating what the Holy Spirit would do to all believers in general.

The second important thing to note about Jesus' statement is *what* the Holy Spirit would do to the apostles during their corporate lifetime. Concerning the Spirit He said: "he shall teach you all things." Jesus thereby indicated that, during the corporate lifetime of the twelve apostles, the Holy Spirit would communicate to that corporate body of men *all* (not just some) of the truth, the knowledge which He would want the Church to have.

This did not mean that each of the twelve apostles would receive *all* of this communication of knowledge from the Holy Spirit individually. John, who was the last of the twelve apostles of Christ to die, received significant revelation from the Holy Spirit years after the other eleven apostles had died (Rev. 1:20; 4:1; 17:3; 21:10). But it did mean that as a corporate body the twelve apostles would receive all the truth, knowledge or revelation which the Church was to have, and that the Holy Spirit would communicate all that truth to that corporate body before its last living member would die.

In addition, Jesus' John 14:26 statement did not mean that the twelve apostles who were gathered with Him in the upper room were the only persons who would have this truth revealed to them by the Holy Spirit. Paul was not in the corporate body of the twelve apostles gathered with Christ in the upper room, and yet he made it clear that he, as an apostle of Christ "born out of due time" (1 Cor. 15:8), and the New Testament prophets also had parts of this truth revealed to them by the Holy Spirit (1 Cor. 2:10–13; Eph. 3:3–5). Jesus' statement did mean that, although Paul and the New Testament prophets would also have parts of this truth revealed to them, the twelve apostles would have all the truth which God wanted the Church to possess revealed to them as a corporate body before that body would pass out of existence.

Since Jesus' John 14:26 statement indicated that the Holy Spirit would reveal all the truth which God wanted the Church to have to the corporate body of twelve apostles before its last living member would die, and since the last living member (John) of the corporate body of twelve apostles died around 100 A.D., then it can be concluded that all of God's revelation to the Church was completed by 100 A.D. Since all of God's revelation to the Church was completed by 100 A.D., and since the revelational gifts of prophecy and knowledge had the God-intended purpose or function of delivering revelation or knowledge of God, then certainly by 100 A.D. there was no further need for those revelational gifts. It can be concluded, then, that God must have done away with the gifts of prophecy and knowledge by 100 A.D.

The second Scripture passage which sheds light on the issue of the duration of the revelational gifts is John 16:12–13. This passage has the same context as the John 14:26 passage. Jesus was speaking to the corporate body of the twelve apostles in the upper room on the night before His crucifixion. Once again Jesus warned the apostles of His impending departure from them to return to the Father (Jn. 16:4–6), and once again He promised that the Comforter, the Holy Spirit, would come to them after His departure (v. 7). Having given this warning and promise, Jesus declared, "I have yet many things to say unto you, but ye cannot bear them now. Nevertheless, when he, the Spirit of truth, is come, he will guide you into all truth; . . .and he will show you things to come" (vv. 12–13).

Once again it is important to note that Jesus addressed these comments specifically to the corporate body of twelve apostles who were gathered with Him that night. He did not address them to all believers in general. In the context (Jn. 15:26–27; 16:4) Jesus made it clear that He was addressing those who had been with Him "from the beginning."

Jesus' statement to the effect that He had many things to say to the apostles, but they could not bear them at that time (v. 12), indicated that He had already taught them so much over the three and one-half years that they had been with Him that the apostles had reached the saturation point. They could not take in any more new truth at that time.

The apostles' inability to take in more truth posed a genuine problem. In light of the fact that Jesus would leave them soon to return to His Father, how would the apostles receive all the new truth that Jesus wanted to communicate to them?

Jesus indicated that the solution to the problem would be the Holy Spirit. When the Holy Spirit would come after Jesus' departure, the Spirit would guide the apostles "into all the truth" (the Greek text has the definite article "the" before the word "truth," v. 13). Jesus explained further how this would work—"for he shall not speak of himself, but whatever he shall hear, that shall he speak" (v. 13). In other words, the Holy Spirit would communicate to the apostles whatever Jesus would speak to Him.

It is important to note that Jesus declared that the Holy Spirit would guide the corporate body of the twelve apostles into *all* the truth, including a knowledge of future events. Apostles and New Testament prophets had the responsibility of communicating to the Church the truth or knowledge which the Holy Spirit communicated to them (1 Cor. 2:7–13; Eph. 3:3–9). This meant, then, that the twelve apostles would be responsible to communicate to the Church all the truth that the Holy Spirit would communicate to them after Jesus' departure to the Father. In light of this responsibility, it can be concluded that, when Jesus declared that the Spirit would guide the apostles into *all* the truth, He was referring to all the truth which He wanted the Church to have.

Thus, in John 16:12–13 Jesus indicated that all the truth, knowledge or revelation which He wanted the Church to have would be delivered to the corporate body of twelve apostles during the corporate lifetime of that group. Since that corporate body came to an end when John, its last living member, died around 100 A.D., then it can be concluded that the Holy Spirit had delivered all the truth that Christ wanted the Church to have by 100 A.D. The Church was not to receive new revelation of truth or knowledge after the end of the apostolic age. Since the Spirit had delivered all the truth or revelation that Christ wanted the Church to have by 100 A.D., then there was no further need for the revelational gifts by that time. Thus, the gifts of prophecy and knowledge must have been put out of existence by 100 A.D.

The third Scripture passage which sheds light on the issue of the duration of the revelational gifts is Ephesians 2:20. In this passage, where Paul drew an analogy between the construction of a building and the construction of the Church, he declared that the apostles and New Testament prophets are the foundation of the Church. The prophets which Paul had in mind were prophets of the New Testament, not Old Testament prophets, for in Ephesians 3:5 Paul indicated that they were contemporaries of the apostles.

Since in his Ephesians 2:20 building analogy Paul declared that the apostles and New Testament prophets are the foundation of the Church, and since the foundation of a building is laid once and for all in the early stages of construction, then it can be concluded that in his analogy Paul implied that the apostles and New Testament prophets were present once and for all in the early stages of the Church. Just as the foundation is not built up to the top of a building, so apostles of Christ and New Testament prophets were not to be present in the Church throughout its history.

Both the apostles of Christ and the New Testament prophets received revelation from the Holy Spirit. In Ephesians 3:4–5 Paul talked about the mystery of Christ which was "now revealed unto his holy apostles and prophets by the Spirit." The fact that both the apostles of Christ and the New Testament prophets received revelation from the Holy Spirit indicates that both groups had been given revelational gifts, such as the gift of prophecy, by the Holy Spirit. It would appear that the gift of prophecy involved two factors: first, the ability to receive revelation directly from the Holy Spirit (1 Cor. 2:10; Eph. 3:3–5), and second, the ability to communicate that revelation with inspired speech to other human beings (1 Cor. 2:13). The second ability guaranteed the accurate, inerrant communication of the revealed truth by the apostles of Christ and New Testament prophets.

In light of what was involved in the gift of prophecy, it can be concluded that it was the possession of the gift of prophecy that made a person a prophet (Rom. 12:3–6; 1 Cor. 12:4, 8–10, 18, 28–29). Thus, God gave the gift of prophecy only to those persons whom He had designated to be prophets. Since the apostles of Christ had been given the gift of prophecy, they too were prophets (cf. Mt. 23:34 where Jesus called His apostles "prophets"; Acts 13:1 where Paul was identified as a prophet; and Rev. 1:3; 10:11; 22:10, 19 which indicated that John was a prophet).

Since God gave the gift of prophecy only to those persons whom He had designated to be prophets (which persons included the apostles of Christ), and since Paul's Ephesians 2:20 analogy implied that the apostles and New Testament prophets were present once and for all in the early stages of the Church, then it can be concluded that the revelational gift of prophecy was present only in the early stages of the Church. The gift of prophecy ceased at the end of the foundational stage of the Church when the apostles and prophets ceased.

Thus, John 14:26; 16:12–13 and Ephesians 2:20 indicate that the revelational gifts (such as prophecy and knowledge) were done away by God by the end of the apostolic age (around 100 A.D.).

An Objection

Some would object to the conclusion which has been drawn from these three biblical passages. They would object by appealing to Joel 2:28 in which God declared, "I will pour out my Spirit upon all flesh; and your sons and your daughters shall prophesy, your old men shall dream dreams, your young men shall see visions." Some would claim that the present-day movement which emphasizes tongues speaking, prophesying and the receiving of revelations from God is the fulfillment of the Joel 2:28 prophecy. Thus, on the basis of Joel 2:28 they would assert that the gift of prophecy and other means of revelation are present in the Church today, and that, therefore, it is wrong to conclude that God ended the revelational gifts around 100 A.D.

There is a significant problem with this approach to Joel 2:28, however. In this passage where God foretold a future time of new revelation through prophesying and other means, He indicated that it would come in conjunction with His pouring out of His Spirit upon *all* flesh (upon all human beings living on the earth).

Two things should be noted concerning this. First, God is not pouring out the Holy Spirit upon *all* human beings living on the earth today. Second, God pours out or gives the Holy Spirit only to believers (Jn. 7:38–39; 14:16–17; Acts 10:44–48; 11:15–18; Rom. 8:9). Since Joel 2:28 referred to a time when God would pour out the Holy Spirit upon all human beings living on the earth, and since God pours out the Spirit only upon believers, then Joel 2:28 was referring to a future time when every human being living on the earth would be a believer. That certainly is not the situation on the earth today.

Between the time that the Joel 2:28 prophecy was delivered and the time that the history of this present earth will end there is only one time period when every human being living on the earth will be a believer. That time period will be during the early foundational stage of the Millennium. Passages such as Matthew 13:37–43, 47–50; 25:31–46 and Luke 17:26–37 indicate that only believers will be allowed to enter the Millennial Kingdom. All living unbelievers will be removed from the earth in judgment in conjunction with Christ's Second Coming.

Other passages teach that children will be born during the Millennium (Jer. 30:19–20; Ezek. 47:22). These children will be born in the same unsaved condition that children are born today. This means, then, that after the early foundational stage of the Millennium, the earth will have unsaved people living on it again. Thus, it is only during the early foundational stage of the Millennium that every human being living on the earth will be a believer. As a result, it is only during the early foundational stage of the Millennium that God will pour out His Spirit upon all flesh and the Joel 2:28 prophecy will be fulfilled.

In Joel 2:28, then, God was indicating that new revelation will come to the earth through prophesying and other means during the early foundational stage of the Millennium. New revelation will come at that time because the early foundational stage of the Millennium will be the beginning part of a new dispensation (a new particular way of God administering His rule over the world). A new dispensation of God's rule places new responsibilities upon human beings on the earth.

Since a new dispensation involves a new way of God administering His rule over the world, and since it places new responsibilities upon human beings on the earth, then each new dispensation requires new revelation. In order to know what is involved in God's new way of administering His rule and their resultant new responsibilities, human beings must have these things revealed to them.

Each new dispensation also requires that the new revelation come during the early foundational stage of the dispensation. If parts of the revelation are not given until late in the dispensation, then those people who live earlier in the dispensation are ignorant of their responsibilities and are in danger of divine judgment for failure to fulfill what God requires in that dispensation.

It is for this reason, then, that God will give the new revelation of the Millennium during the early foundational stage of that dispensation (during the time that God will be able to pour out the Holy Spirit upon all human beings living on the earth). It is also for this reason that, during the early foundational stage of this present dispensation (when apostles of Christ and New Testament prophets were present in the Church), God gave the Church all the revelation that He wanted it to have and then did away with the revelational gifts by 100 A.D.

THE GIFT OF TONGUES AND THE OLD TESTAMENT

Introduction

In 1 Corinthians 13:8 the Apostle Paul, writing under the supernatural influence of the Holy Spirit, declared the following: "Love never faileth; but . . . whether there be tongues, they shall cease." Since the Holy Spirit moved Paul to make this declaration in the midst of his most extensive discourse on spiritual gifts, it would appear that the apostle's statement was intended to communicate the following truth: In contrast with love which is permanent (never faileth), the gift of tongues would be temporary in duration (shall cease).

In spite of the fact that Paul taught the temporary duration of the gift of tongues, nowhere in 1 Corinthians 13 did he indicate *when* that gift would cease. One must look elsewhere in Scripture in order to learn how long God intended tongues to last.

1 Corinthians 14:22 And Old Testament Background

In an earlier chapter, the following significant principle concerning spiritual gifts was noted: The duration of a spiritual gift is determined by its purpose or function. A gift will continue to exist until it fulfills its God-intended purpose or function. Once it fulfills that purpose or function, the gift is no longer necessary, and God does away with it.

In light of this principle, in order to learn how long God intended the gift of tongues to last, one must search the

Scriptures to find the God-intended purpose or function of that gift.

There is only one biblical passage which clearly indicates the purpose or function of the gift of tongues. That passage is 1 Corinthians 14:22 where the Apostle Paul drew the following conclusion: "Wherefore tongues are for a sign, not to them that believe, but to them that believe not."

Several significant things should be noted concerning Paul's statement in this passage. First, the combination of Greek words which are translated "are for" in Paul's statement was used in New Testament times to indicate "the vocation, use, or end" which something was to serve.[1] In addition, the word which is translated "for" was used by Paul to denote "appointment."[2] Thus, in 1 Corinthians 14:22 Paul was drawing a conclusion concerning the divinely appointed vocation, use or end which the gift of tongues was to serve. In other words, he was indicating the God-intended purpose or function of that gift. No other biblical passage related to tongues uses such terms which indicate the divinely appointed purpose or function of that gift.

Second, Paul's statement indicated that God appointed tongues to function as a sign. Thus, God intended tongues to be a sign gift. He did not intend it to be an edification gift by itself.

Third, Paul's statement also indicated that God appointed tongues to be a sign to unbelievers, not to believers. Thus, God intended the gift of tongues by itself to be exercised for the benefit of unbelievers, not for the benefit of believers. In order for that divine intention to be fulfilled, the gift had to be exercised in public, not in private, by the believer who possessed the gift.

These three things which have been noted concerning Paul's statement prompt two significant questions. First, God intended the gift of tongues to be a sign of what to unbelievers? Second, did God intend tongues to be a sign to all unbelievers in general or to a specific group of unbelievers?

The opening word of Paul's 1 Corinthians 14:22 statement gives a clue concerning where the answers to these questions can be found. The word "wherefore" indicates that Paul based his conclusion concerning the purpose of the gift of tongues (v. 22) upon what he had just stated in the preceding verse (v. 21). In verse 21 Paul had stated the following: "In the law it is written, With men of other tongues and other lips will I speak unto this people; and yet for all that will they not hear me, saith the Lord."

In verse 21 Paul quoted from Isaiah 28:11–12. The context of Isaiah 28:11–12 emphasized the tragic situation which existed in Israel during Isaiah's time. Through Isaiah the prophet, His spokesman, God had told the leaders of Israel what they should do in order to give the people of Israel rest from conquest and oppression by foreign powers (v. 12). Isaiah spoke God's word very clearly and repeatedly, "precept upon precept; line upon line" (vv. 10, 13), so that the leaders of Israel could not miss the message.

In spite of Isaiah's clear, methodical way of presenting God's message, the leaders "would not hear" (v. 12). They ridiculed the fact that God's prophet spokesman was trying to teach them, the leaders of the nation, knowledge. They complained that, in so doing, Isaiah was treating them as immature, little children (v. 9). They mocked his clear, repetitive method of presenting God's Word (v. 10). In other words, they willfully rejected God's message and prophet messenger.

Because these leaders of Israel rejected God's message in spite of its clear, methodical presentation by God's prophet messenger, God declared that He would speak to them in another way—"with stammering lips and another tongue will he speak to this people" (v. 11). What did God mean by this declaration? He meant that He would speak to these rebellious Jews through judgment—the judgment of conquest and oppression by foreigners whose language the Jews would not understand. As the Jews would be forced to listen to this foreign language of their oppressors, it would be a sign to them that they were under the judgment of God and that God was working with those who spoke the foreign language.

Several other Old Testament passages demonstrate that this is what God meant by His Isaiah 28:11 statement. In Jeremiah 5 God accused Israel and Judah of treacherous dealings against Him (v. 11). They had denied the truthfulness of what God had said about them through His prophets (v. 12). They had accused God's prophets of being windbags who proclaimed something other than the true Word of God (v. 13). In other words, these Jews willfully rejected God's message and prophet messengers.

Because of this treachery by the Jews, God said that He would do the following to them: "I will bring a nation upon you from far, O house of Israel, saith the Lord; it is a mighty nation, it is an ancient nation, a nation whose language thou knowest not, neither understandest what they say" (v. 15). Thus, here again, because of their rejection of His message and prophet messengers, God declared that He would judge the Jews through conquest and oppression by foreigners whose language the Jews would not understand.

Very early in Israel's history, God mapped out the future course of His dealings with that nation in another significant Old Testament passage. In Deuteronomy 28:1–14 God declared that, if the people of Israel would listen to and obey His Word, which was delivered through Moses His prophet (v. 1), He would bless them more than any other nation on the earth. But in Deuteronomy 28:15–68 God warned that, if they would not listen to and obey His Word, which was delivered through Moses His prophet (v. 15), He would curse them severely. One of the curses which God promised to bring upon Israel was this: "The Lord shall bring a nation against thee from far, from the end of the earth, as swift as the eagle flieth; a nation whose tongue thou shalt not understand" (v. 49). Once again God associated the speaking of a foreign language, which the Jews could not understand, with His judgment of the Jews because of their rejection of His message delivered through His prophet.

In Deuteronomy 28:46 God made the following statement concerning His promised curses of Israel: "And they shall be upon thee for a sign and for a wonder, and upon thy seed forever." This declaration by God is most significant for several reasons. First, it indicates that God intended His promised curses upon Israel to function as a sign—a sign to the effect that God was intervening into the course of history to judge the Jews. Since one of God's promised curses was the speaking of a foreign language which the Jews could not understand (v.

49), this means that God intended the speaking of such a foreign language to function as a sign of His judgment.

Second, in light of the fact that the curses of Deuteronomy 28 were promised by God specifically for the people of Israel, God indicated that those curses would function as a sign specifically for the Israelites. Since one of those promised curses was the speaking of a foreign language which the Jews could not understand, this means that God intended the speaking of such a foreign language to function as a judgment sign only for the Jews. He never intended such speaking to function as a judgment sign for the Gentiles.

Third, in His Deuteronomy 28:46 statement God indicated that His promised curses of Deuteronomy 28 would function as a sign of God's judgment for the seed of Israel forever. In other words, they would function as a sign of God's judgment to every generation of Jews which would be exposed to those curses as the result of rejecting God's message which had been delivered to that generation by God's prophet. Since one of those promised curses was the speaking of a foreign language which the Jews could not understand, this means that God intended the speaking of such a language to function as a sign of God's judgment to every generation of Jews which He judges for rejecting God's message delivered to it by God's prophet. Because of this, as noted earlier in Isaiah 28 and Jeremiah 5, since the Jews of Isaiah's and Jeremiah's times rejected God's message and prophet messengers, God declared that He would speak to them in another way—through judgment. A sign of this judgment to those rebellious Jews would be as follows: they would be forced to listen to a foreign language which they could not understand.

In light of this meaning of Isaiah 28:11, and in light of the fact that Paul used Isaiah 28:11 as the basis of his conclusion concerning the God-intended purpose of the gift of tongues in the Church, a significant question must be asked at this point. Since God made His Isaiah 28:11 statement several centuries before He gave the gift of tongues to the Church, what possible connection could there be between His Old Testament statement and the gift of tongues in the New Testament Church?

41

Endnotes

[1] William F. Arndt and F. Wilbur Gingrich, "eis," "eimi," *A Greek-English Lexicon of the New Testament* (4th rev. ed.; Chicago: The University of Chicago Press, 1957), pp. 228, 224.

[2] Albrecht Oepke, "eis," *Theological Dictionary of the New Testament*, Vol. II (Grand Rapids: Wm. B. Eerdmans Publishing Co., 1964), p. 428.

THE CONNECTION OF ISAIAH 28:11 TO THE GIFT OF TONGUES

Introduction

In 1 Corinthians 14:21–22 the Apostle Paul based his conclusion concerning the purpose of the gift of tongues upon a statement found in Isaiah 28:11. The fact that Paul did this indicates that the Old Testament provided background for understanding the purpose of the gift of tongues in the New Testament Church.

The previous chapter on spiritual gifts examined this background and noted the fact that Isaiah 28:11 expressed a principle which was developed in the Old Testament. The principle was as follows: every generation of Jews to which God sends a prophet spokesman and which God judges for rejecting His message and prophet spokesman will be forced to listen to foreign language which it cannot understand as a sign of that judgment.

In light of this principle expressed in Isaiah 28:11 and the fact that Paul used it as the basis of his conclusion concerning the purpose of the gift of tongues in the Church, the previous chapter concluded with the following question: Since the Isaiah 28:11 statement was made several centuries before God gave the gift of tongues to the Church, what connection was there between His Old Testament statement and the gift of tongues in the New Testament Church?

This chapter will deal with that question.

The Purpose of the Gift of Tongues

An explanation will indicate the connection between Isaiah 28:11 and the gift of tongues. God's ultimate prophet spokesman whom He sent to Israel was His own Son, Jesus Christ. Jesus indicated that He was a prophet (Mt. 13:57; Lk. 13:33; Jn. 4:43–44). He repeatedly claimed to be God's spokesman, sent by God to speak His message (Jn. 7:16–18; 8:26, 28–29, 38, 40, 42; 12:44–45, 49–50; 14:10; 17:8, 14). He insinuated that His words and deeds were greater than those of the Old Testament prophets (Mt. 13:17; Lk. 10:24).

Other persons recognized that Jesus was a prophet spokesman of God (Mt. 21:11, 46; Lk. 7:16; 24:19; Jn. 4:19; 6:14; 7:40; 9:17). The writer of the Epistle to the Hebrews testified to that effect when he wrote, "God, who at sundry times and in diverse manners spoke in time past unto the fathers by the prophets, Hath in these last days spoken unto us by his Son" (Heb. 1:1–2). The writer of Hebrews then made statements about Jesus which clearly indicated that He was God's ultimate prophet spokesman, far superior to other prophets (1:2–12).

Moses foretold the fact that God would send a significant prophet to Israel. He declared that God would place His words in that prophet's mouth. As a result, that prophet would speak to the people of Israel all that God would command Him to say. Moses warned that the Israelites should listen to that prophet (Dt. 18:15, 18). By Jesus' time the Jews called this prophet to whom Moses referred "that prophet" or "the prophet" (Jn. 1:21; 6:14; 7:40). These designations indicate that the Jews understood that this prophet would be special, more significant than other prophets. Peter indicated that Jesus was this special prophet (Acts 3:20–22).

In light of the Old Testament principle expressed in Isaiah 28:11 and the fact that Jesus was God's ultimate prophet spokesman to Israel, a parable which He taught was most significant. Jesus talked about a man who planted a vineyard, turned its care over to tenant farmers, and then took a long trip. When the harvest time came, the man sent his servants to the tenants to receive his share of the fruit. The tenants beat and killed the owner's servants. Being frustrated with the wrong actions of the tenants toward his servants, the owner sent his own son to the vineyard. He thought that the tenants would respect his son more than his servants. However, the tenants gave the owner's son the same treatment as his servants—they killed him. When the owner of the vineyard returned from his trip, he severely judged the original tenants (Mt. 21:33-41).

In this parable, the owner of the vineyard represented God. The vineyard represented God's program of operation in the world, particularly as that program centered in the nation of Israel in Old Testament times (v. 43). The tenant farmers represented the spiritual leaders of Israel. The owner's servants represented God's Old Testament prophet spokesmen. The owner's son represented Jesus Christ.

In light of these representations, it can be concluded that Jesus taught this parable in order to communicate the following concepts to the spiritual leaders of Israel in His day (v. 45). When God planted His program of operation in the world in Old Testament times, He centered that program primarily in the nation of Israel as His base of operation. He entrusted the care of His program of operation to the spiritual leaders of Israel. They were to nurture God's program in such a way that it would produce the kind of results that God intended it to produce. This nurturing would involve the spiritual leaders guiding the people of Israel in obedience to God's Word as that Word would be proclaimed by God's prophet spokesmen.

But, when God sent His prophet spokesmen to Israel with His message in Old Testament times, the spiritual leaders led the Jews to reject God's message and prophet spokesmen. In many instances, the spiritual leaders instigated the beating and killing of God's prophets.

Since Israel killed God's Old Testament prophets and rejected His message delivered by those prophets, God finally sent His ultimate prophet spokesman, His own Son, Jesus Christ, to the nation with His message. Since Jesus was God's Son, His ultimate prophet spokesman, the spiritual leaders of Israel should respect Him more than God's Old Testament prophets. However, the spiritual leaders would lead the Jews to give

God's Son the same treatment as His Old Testament prophets were given—they would kill Him and reject God's message delivered by Him.

Because Israel would kill God's Son and reject God's message through Him, God would severely judge that nation and its spiritual leaders.

These concepts which were communicated by Jesus through this parable were presented in non-parabolic form on other occasions by Jesus and other persons. Moses warned that those Jews who would not listen to God's message spoken by the significant prophet whom God would send would be judged by God (Dt. 18:19). When Peter applied Moses' prophecy concerning that prophet to Jesus, he repeated Moses' warning (Acts 3:20–23). Stephen severely accused the spiritual elders of Israel in his day of killing Jesus, God's just One, just as their ancestors killed God's Old Testament prophets (Acts 7:51–52).

Jesus warned that those who would reject Him and His message would be judged (Jn. 12:48). He declared that He must suffer many things and be rejected by the generation of Jews which saw and heard Him (Lk. 17:25). He stated that that generation of Jews would be judged because it did not listen to Him in spite of the fact that He was greater than the Prophet Jonah and Solomon (Mt. 12:41–42). Several times He called that generation "wicked" and "perverse" (Mt. 12:45; 17:17). Jesus' most ominous warning was to the effect that the judgment for the killing of all God's Old Testament prophets (from Abel to Zechariah) would come upon that generation of Jews which saw and heard Him, because that generation would do the same thing that their ancestors did—kill God's prophet spokesmen (Mt. 23:29–38; Lk. 11:47–51; 13:33–35).

Jesus indicated that a major part of the judgment upon that generation would consist of the siege and destruction of Jerusalem and its inhabitants (Lk. 19:41–44).

In light of these concepts concerning the relationship of God's judgment to Israel's treatment of God's Old Testament prophets and His ultimate prophet spokesman, His own Son, several parallels can be seen. First, just as generations of Jews of Old Testament times rejected God's message and killed His prophet spokesmen who delivered that message, so the generation of Jews of Jesus' day rejected God's message and killed His ultimate prophet spokesman, His Son Jesus.

Second, just as God judged the Old Testament generations of Jews for rejecting His message and killing His prophet spokesmen, so God judged the generation of Jews of Jesus' day for rejecting His message and killing His ultimate prophet spokesman, His Son Jesus. This latter judgment will be described later.

A third parallel is implied by the concepts examined earlier. Just as God used the element of foreign language which the Jews could not understand as a sign for the Old Testament generations of Jews who rejected His message and killed His prophet spokesmen, so God used the element of foreign language which the Jews could not understand as a sign for the generation of Jews of Jesus' day who rejected His message and killed His ultimate prophet spokesman, His Son Jesus. In both instances, God used the element of foreign language as a sign that those Jews were subject to the judgment of God and that God was working with those who spoke the foreign language.

The validity of this third parallel is substantiated by Deuteronomy 28:46, 49 where, as noted earlier, God indicated that the curse of foreign language which the Jews cannot understand would be a sign of His judgment to every generation of Jews which rejects God's message and His prophet spokesmen sent to it.

These three parallels explain the connection which Paul made in 1 Corinthians 14:21–22 between God's Isaiah 28:11 statement and the gift of tongues in the New Testament Church. Paul was indicating that the gift of tongues in the New Testament Church had the same God-intended purpose or function toward the generation of Jews of Jesus' time as did the foreign language of Isaiah 28:11 toward the generation of Jews of Isaiah's time. In other words, Paul concluded that the gift of tongues in the New Testament Church had the God-intended purpose of functioning as a sign to that wicked, unbelieving generation of Jews which had heard and seen Jesus Christ, but then killed Him. God purposed the gift of tongues to be a sign to the effect that that generation of Jews was subject to the severe judgment of God and that God was now working in a unique sense with those (the Church) who exercised the gift of tongues.

This God-intended purpose for the gift of tongues has a significant implication concerning the issue of the duration of that gift. That implication will be examined in the next chapter.

THE CESSATION OF
THE GIFT OF TONGUES

Introduction

In 1 Corinthians 14:21–22, the Apostle Paul indicated a connection between Isaiah 28:11 and the gift of tongues in the New Testament Church. The previous chapter examined that connection and Paul's conclusion concerning the purpose of the gift of tongues. Paul concluded that God purposed tongues to be a sign to that wicked, unbelieving generation of Jews which heard and saw Jesus Christ but then killed Him—a sign to the effect that that generation of Jews was subject to the severe judgment of God and that God was now working in a unique sense with those (the Church) who exercised the gift of tongues.

The Verification of This Purpose

That this was the God-intended purpose for the gift of tongues in the New Testament Church is verified by what happened when the Church was born on the day of Pentecost (Acts 2). God brought the Church into existence and gave it the gift of tongues just 53 days after the generation of Jews of Jesus' time had Him killed. On that day of Pentecost, the Church exercised the gift of tongues for the first time in the presence of thousands of Jews who belonged to that generation and who had gathered to Jerusalem from many nations to observe Pentecost (vv. 4–6). After the tongues speaking had drawn the attention of the Jews to the tongues speakers, Peter spoke to the crowd of Jews (v. 14). He addressed them as "Ye men of Israel" (v. 22) and accused them of killing Jesus of Nazareth, whom God had clearly demonstrated to be the Messiah, had resurrected from the dead, and had exalted at His right hand in Heaven (vv. 22, 32–33, 36). Having thereby pressed home the fact that their generation had killed God's ultimate prophet spokesman, Peter issued the following warning to these Jews: "Save yourselves from this crooked generation" (v. 40). That warning implied that that generation of Jews was heading for judgment because of what it had done to Jesus. It is significant that Peter issued such a warning in the context of the Church receiving and exercising the gift of tongues for the first time. Thus, on the first day of its existence, the gift of tongues was associated with the concept of God's judgment coming on the generation of Jews which killed God's ultimate prophet spokesman.

Three observations should be made concerning what happened on Pentecost (Acts 2). First, just as the Old Testament principle which was expressed in Isaiah 28:11 involved the speaking of actual human language of an earthly nation, so the gift of tongues on Pentecost involved the speaking of actual human languages of earthly nations (vv. 6–11). The Spirit gave the believers the ability to speak human languages which they had never learned. The believers were not speaking ecstatic utterances.

Second, even though each Jew on Pentecost could understand what was said when the tongues speakers spoke the language which was native to his own country, he could not understand when the tongues speakers spoke the other languages which were foreign to his own country. For example, a Jew who had come to Jerusalem from Phrygia (v. 10) could understand what was said when the tongues speakers spoke his Phrygian language, but he could not understand when they spoke the languages of Arabia (v. 11) and Parthia (v. 9). Thus, just as the Old Testament principle which was expressed in Isaiah 28:11 involved language which was foreign to the Jews, so the gift of tongues on Pentecost involved languages which were foreign to the Jews.

Third, some believe that the purpose of the gift of tongues on Pentecost was evangelism. According to this view, the Spirit enabled the believers to speak the languages of all the

Jews present so that they could communicate the gospel in all those languages. There are problems with this view, however. First, Acts 2 does not state that the gospel was communicated through the tongues speaking. It does state that the tongues speakers spoke "the wonderful works of God" (v. 11). Perhaps that involved a declaration of the gospel, but no one can be certain of that. Second, if the gospel had already been communicated to the Jews through the tongues speaking, then why did Peter declare the gospel to the same Jews after the tongues speaking had stopped on Pentecost? The major part of Peter's message would have been unnecessary if the gospel had already been given immediately before he preached. Third, the gift of tongues was not needed for the purpose of evangelism in New Testament times. The Greek language had become a universal trade language by those times. It would have been understood by the Jews who had come to Jerusalem from different nations. Thus, there was no language barrier to the presentation of the gospel on Pentecost. The Jews who were there would have understood a Greek language declaration of that message. If tongues were necessary to evangelize all the Jews on Pentecost, then how did Peter present the gospel to them after the tongues speaking had stopped on that day? It seems obvious that Peter preached to the crowd of Jews in one language—probably the Greek language.

In light of the connection which Paul made in 1 Corinthians 14:21–22 between God's Isaiah 28:11 statement and the gift of tongues in the New Testament Church, another observation should be made. Since the Old Testament principle expressed in Isaiah 28:11 involved the speaking of actual human language of an earthly nation, and since Paul based his conclusion concerning the purpose of the gift of tongues upon the principle expressed in Isaiah 28 and presented that conclusion in his discussion of tongues in 1 Corinthians 14, it would appear that the tongues to which Paul referred in 1 Corinthians 14 also involved the speaking of actual human languages rather than ecstatic utterances. In line with this observation is the fact that in 1 Corinthians 14 (as well as in chapters 12 and 13) Paul consistently used the same word for tongues as was used by Luke in

Acts 2 for the tongues of Pentecost (which, as noted earlier, were also actual human languages in line with the principle expressed in Isaiah 28).

The Duration of the Gift of Tongues

Paul concluded that God purposed the gift of tongues in the New Testament Church to be a sign specifically to that generation of Jews which killed Jesus Christ—a sign to the effect that that generation of Jews was subject to the severe judgment of God and that God was now working in a unique sense with those (the Church) who spoke the tongues. Jesus foretold that the judgment upon that generation would include the siege and destruction of Jerusalem and its inhabitants (Lk. 19:41–44). The judgment came in the form of The Jewish War which the Jews waged against Rome in the land of Israel from May, 66 A.D. to May, 73 A.D. The Romans responded to the Jewish revolt with a vengeance. They systematically destroyed or captured the revolting cities. In fulfillment of Jesus' prophecy, the Romans besieged and destroyed Jerusalem and the Temple, with the final destruction of the city taking place on September 26, 70 A.D. During the course of the war, great multitudes of Jews were tortured and slaughtered, many by crucifixion. Thousands suffered and died from the horrors of famine and pestilence. Large numbers were captured and sold into slavery.[1] Josephus, the famous Jewish historian who wrote an extensive eyewitness account of the war, recorded the number of those Jews who died or were captured. According to one scholar, the totals of the numbers recorded by Josephus were as follows: 1,356,460 Jews killed from the beginning to the close of the war, and 101,700 taken prisoner.[2]

Josephus recognized that the destruction of Jerusalem was God's judgment because of the wickedness of the generation of Jews which was in that city. He wrote: "I believe that, had the Romans delayed their punishment of these villains, the city would have been swallowed up by the earth, or overwhelmed with a flood, or, like Sodom, consumed with fire from heaven. For the generation which was in it was far more ungodly than the men on whom these punishments had in former times fallen. By their madness the whole nation came to be ruined."[3]

Eusebius Pamphilus, who lived around 265—339 A.D., served as bishop of Caesarea in the land of Israel and wrote a significant work tracing the history of the Church from its beginning to 324 A.D.[4], wrote the following significant statements concerning The Jewish War:

> *The whole body, however, of the church at Jerusalem, having been commanded by a divine revelation, given to men of approved piety there before the war, removed from the city, and dwelt at a certain town beyond the Jordan, called Pella. Here, those that believed in Christ, having removed from Jerusalem, as if holy men had entirely abandoned the royal city itself, and the whole land of Judea; the divine justice, for their crimes against Christ and his apostles, finally overtook them, totally destroying the whole generation of these evildoers from the earth.[5]*

> *For it was indeed just, that in those very days in which they had inflicted sufferings upon the Saviour and benefactor of all men, the Christ of God, destruction should overtake them, thus shut up as in a prison, as an exhibition of the divine justice . . . .The divine vengeance did not long delay to visit them for their iniquity against the Christ of God.[6]*

These statements by Eusebius are significant for two reasons. First, they indicate that the early Church regarded the horrors of The Jewish War to be God's judgment upon the generation of Jews which had killed Christ. Second, they also indicate that this judgment *did* not fall upon the Jews who had believed in Jesus, even though they were part of that same generation.

Both of these reasons correspond precisely with what has been noted concerning Paul's expressed purpose of the gift of tongues in the New Testament Church. Tongues had the purpose of being a sign of God's judgment to the unbelievers of the generation of Jews which had killed Christ. It was not a sign of judgment to the believers of that generation.

In an earlier chapter it was noted that the duration of a spiritual gift is determined by its purpose or function. Once a gift fulfills its purpose or function, it is no longer necessary, and

God does away with it. In light of this principle and the purpose of the gift of tongues in the New Testament Church, it can be concluded that the gift of tongues fulfilled its purpose or function by the time God poured out all the judgment of which the tongues were to be a sign. Since the gift of tongues was to be a sign of judgment to the generation of Jews which killed Christ, and since that judgment came in the form of The Jewish War from 66 to 73 A.D., it can be concluded that the biblical gift of tongues fulfilled its purpose or function by 73 A.D. and, therefore, ceased around that time.

Endnotes

[1] Josephus, *The Essential Writings*, trans. and ed. by Paul L. Maier (Grand Rapids: Kregel Publications, 1988), pp. 281–282.

[2] Henry Hart Milman, *The History of the Jews*, Vol. II, p. 388; quoted by Philip Schaff, *History of the Christian Church*, Vol. I (Grand Rapids: Wm. B. Eerdmans Publishing Co., 1975), p. 400, footnote 2.

[3] Josephus, *The Jewish War*, Book V, Chapter 13, Section 6 quoted by Philip Schaff, History of the Christian Church, Vol. I., p. 399.

[4] Earle E. Cairns, *Christianity Through The Centuries*, second revised edition (Grand Rapids: Zondervan Publishing House, 1981), p. 143.

[5] *The Ecclesiastical History Of Eusebius Pamphilus*, Book III, Chapter V, trans. by Christian Frederick Cruse (Grand Rapids: Baker Book House, 1955), p. 86.

[6] Ibid., p. 87.

CONCLUDING CONSIDERATIONS

The Meaning of "Perfect" in 1 Corinthians 13:10

1 Corinthians 13:10 says, "But when that which is perfect is come, then that which is in part shall be done away." In an earlier chapter we saw that this verse is not talking about spiritual gifts being done away. The expression "in part" is not referring to spiritual gifts. Instead, it is referring back to the partial revelation or knowledge of God which came through revelational gifts. Thus, verse 10 is declaring that, when the "perfect" comes, this partial revelation or knowledge of God, which came through the revelational gifts, will be done away.

The word translated "perfect" in verse 10 means "whole," "complete," "total."[1] It is the complement of "in part." It is referring to the same thing as "in part," but the whole, complete complement of what is "in part." Thus, since "in part" is referring to a partial revelation or knowledge of God, then "perfect" is referring to the total, complete revelation or knowledge of God.

In light of this, verse 10 is stating that, when the total, complete revelation or knowledge of God comes, then the partial revelation or knowledge of God, which came through the revelational gifts, will be done away (done away in the sense of no longer being partial. Certainly the total, complete revelation or knowledge of God will contain all that the partial contained but much more).

Since verse 12 draws a contrast between present partial knowledge and much fuller future knowledge, it appears that verse 10 is also drawing a contrast between two levels of knowledge—total, complete in contrast with partial. Verse 12 says, "For now we see through a glass, darkly; but then face to face; now I know in part; but then shall I know even as also I am known."

But what specific identifications are to be assigned to the partial and complete bodies of revelation or knowledge? It appears that the partial is the revelation or knowledge of God which came through the revelational gifts and is now contained in the Scriptures, and the "perfect" is the total, complete revelation or knowledge of God which will come to the believer in the future when he is face to face with the Lord. Commenting on 1 Corinthians 13:10, 12, Gerhard Delling indicated that revelational gifts "do not give full knowledge of God. This will be granted to the Christian only with the immediacy of face-to-face."[2]

The Bible certainly contains all the truth or knowledge God intends mankind to have while in our present mortal state during this present age in which we live. It gives us everything we need to know in this life about God, how to be saved and live a godly life, and His purposes for history, mankind, Israel, and the Church. In its entirety it is God's Word to mankind and is divinely intended to have full authority over what people believe and do. But in the future, when we are face-to-face with the Lord, we shall receive even more revelation or knowledge of God suitable for life beyond this present age.

The conclusions that the "partial" is the revelation or knowledge of God which is now contained in the Scriptures, and the "perfect" is the total, complete revelation or knowledge of God which will come to the believer in the future when he is face-to-face with the Lord are based on the following concepts:

1. In 1 Corinthians 13:12 Paul wrote, "For now we see through a glass, darkly; but then face to face; now I know in part; but then shall I know even as also I am known." Paul thereby drew a contrast between partial knowledge that one has from looking at the image of a person reflected in a mirror and complete knowledge that one has from a face-to-face relationship with that person. A mirror reflection reveals significant things about that person, but a face-to-face meeting reveals far more.

A face-to-face meeting can answer many questions that a mirror reflection leaves unanswered concerning a person.

2. James indicated that looking into the Scriptures is analogous to looking in a mirror (James 1:22-25). In 2 Corinthians 3:18 Paul implied the same analogy when he wrote, "But we all, with open face beholding as in a glass the glory of the Lord, are changed into the same image from glory to glory, even as by the Spirit of the Lord." As Christians look into the Scriptures, those Scriptures reflect the glorious moral image of God. They reveal significant knowledge concerning the holy nature of God. The Holy Spirit uses that biblical revelation to conform believers progressively in stages to that moral image.

3. Gerhard Kittel asserts that Paul used "the figure of the mirror" to express the same thought in 2 Corinthians 3:18 and 1 Corinthians 13:12. Both refer to what is now present-- the partial revelation or knowledge of God.[3] Since both 2 Corinthians 3:18 and 1 Corinthians 13:12 use the figure of the mirror to refer to the partial revelation or knowledge of God now present, and since in 2 Corinthians 3:18 Paul implies that looking into the Scriptures is analogous to looking in a mirror, it appears that Paul was indicating that the partial is the revelation or knowledge of God which is now contained in the Scriptures.

4. The Scriptures were written by valid prophets of God (those who possessed revelational gifts—the God-given abilities to receive revelation or knowledge directly from God and to present that revelation or knowledge in inspired, inerrant form—1 Cor. 2:6–13; Eph. 3:2–5) (this included the apostles). Thus, the Scriptures are the result of the God-given revelational gifts which gave a partial revelation or knowledge of God to man.

5. Although the Scriptures were written in inspired, inerrant from and contained all the revelation or knowledge that God intended and that the Church needed, they did not contain all the knowledge that is true concerning God. Since the world is not large enough to contain written records of all that Jesus did in just 3 1/2 years of ministry (Jn. 21:25), then certainly the Bible does not contain all the knowledge that is true concerning the eternal, infinite, omnipotent God. This indicates that

the Bible contains a partial revelation or knowledge of God.

6. In 2 Corinthians 12:4 Paul refers to revelation or knowledge to which he was exposed when he was caught up to the third heaven (v. 2), but he makes it clear that no human is allowed to relate that knowledge to other humans. In light of this restriction, it must be concluded that he was exposed to revelation or knowledge which is not recorded in the Bible. Once again the implication is that the Bible contains a partial revelation or knowledge of God.

7. 1 Corinthians 13:12 indicates that believers will not be exposed to the full, complete revelation or knowledge of God until they are face-to-face with the Lord in the future. This means that now we possess a partial revelation or knowledge of God. Indeed, what we have now is sufficient for salvation and godly living, but we shall know much more about God and His ways when we are face-to-face with the Lord. Job said to the Lord, "I have heard of thee by the hearing of the ear: but now mine eye seeth thee. Wherefore I abhor *myself*, and repent in dust and ashes" (Job 42:5–6).

8. In 2 Peter 1:19–21 Peter indicates that the Scriptures (which came through prophecy—through the revelational gifts) are like a light (an oil-burning lamp) shining in a dark place. Believers had better pay attention to them, because their ultimate source is God, and, therefore, they are the divinely authoritative guide revealing the path which believers are to walk during this present age of spiritual darkness. But Peter declares that believers are to pay this heed to the Scriptures "*until* the day dawn, and the day star arise in your hearts" (until they see the Lord). The implication of Peter's statements is this: Just as the sun (a star) gives off far more light than an oil lamp, so the face-to-face meeting with the Lord in the future will expose the believer to far more revelation and knowledge of God than the Scriptures do now. The Scriptures contain a partial revelation or knowledge of God absolutely essential for this present age, but the full, complete revelation or knowledge of God will come to believers when they are face-to-face with the Lord. It appears that this passage by Peter is parallel to Paul's in 1 Corinthians 13.

1 Corinthians 14: 23–25

In verse 23 Paul referred to two classes of unsaved people—the "unlearned" and the "unbelievers." The unlearned were people who had not learned anything about Christianity. Many of the Gentiles in Greece were ignorant concerning Christianity at this time. The unbelievers were those who had a knowledge of Christianity, but rejected it.

Paul stated that, if people from these two classes of the unsaved were to come into a church service out of curiosity and were to hear *all* the believers speak in tongues without interpretation into their language, they would conclude that the Christians were mad ("out of their minds"). The unlearned would conclude, "If this is what Christianity is, we want no part of it." The unbelievers would conclude, "This just proves all the more that we were right to reject Christianity."

In order to demonstrate the fact that prophecy was a sign to believers that God was working with them (see v. 22), in verses 24–25 Paul signified that, if the unlearned (people who were ignorant concerning Christianity) and unbelievers (those who had a knowledge of Christianity, but rejected it) were to come into a church service and were to hear all the believers prophesy, they would come under strong conviction, would get converted, and would testify that God was surely with the Christians.

How would this happen? Through the gift of prophecy, God would reveal to the Christians the sins and pasts of these visitors (cf. Jn. 4:16–19). Then, as the Christians would declare the sins and pasts of these visitors in their language that they could understand, the visitors would be devastatingly and totally exposed for what they were.

In light of the purposes and effects of tongues and prophecy, believers were to pursue the gift of prophecy rather than tongues to be exercised in a church service (see vv. 1–5).

1 Corinthians 13:1–3

Paul used the Greek third class condition in all the conditional clauses of vv.1–3. The Greek third class condition deals with the future and implies uncertainty.[4] Thus, Paul was not saying that he actually did all these things. But he was saying that, even if he were to do such things in the future, he would be way off base if he were to do them apart from love. David K. Lowery points out that Paul's statement about speaking with the tongues of angels is "a statement of hyperbole."[5] According to The American College Dictionary, hyperbole is "obvious exaggeration, for effect; an extravagant statement not intended to be understood literally."[6]

Endnotes

1 Gerhard Delling, "teleios," *Theological Dictionary of the New Testament*, Vol. VIII (Grand Rapids: Wm. B. Eerdmans Publishing Company, 1972), pp. 74-75.

2 Ibid., p. 75.

3 Gerhard Kittel, "katoptridzomai," *Theological Dictionary of the New Testament*, Vol. II (Grand Rapids: Wm. B. Eerdmans Publishing Company, 1964), p. 696.

4 H.E. Dana and Julius R. Mantey, *A Manual Grammar of the Greek New Testament* (New York: The Macmillan Company, 1927), p. 290.

5 David K. Lowery, "1 Corinthians," in *The Bible Knowledge Commentary*, New Testament Edition, ed. by John F. Walvoord and Roy B. Zuck (Wheaton, IL: Victor Books, 1983), p. 535.

6 *The American College Dictionary*, Text Edition (New York:Harper & Brothers Publishers, 1948), p. 594.